Creativity

A coloring collection

by Rachel Parker

ISBN-13: 978-1517224479
Printed by CreateSpace, an Amazon company
www.CreateSpace.com/5276893

Dedicated to my wonderful boys
Will and Liam...My inspiration.

LAUGH
FATE
PEACE
LOVE

LAUGH

Peace
Hope
Love

www.ingramcontent.com/pod-product-compliance
Lightning Source LLC
Chambersburg PA
CBHW081234280526
45787CB00006B/2660
* 9 7 8 1 5 1 7 2 2 4 4 7 9 *